WINNING the Money Game

A Rule Book to Achieving Financial Success for Young People

ADAM CARROLL • CHAD CARDEN

WINNING the Money Game

A Rule Book to Achieving Financial Success for Young People

Published by
National Financial Educators, Inc
1031 Office Park Road, Suite 1
West Des Moines, IA 50265
(515) 223-2343
www.nationalfinancialeducators.com

Authors:
Adam Carroll (www.adamspeaks.com)
Chad Carden (www.chadcardengroup.com)

Advance Praise for
Winning The Money Game

"Adam and Chad have outlined exactly what it takes to put yourself on the path to winning the game we all play with money. If you want to soar with the eagles, you MUST read and understand the "rules" described in this book."

- **Dr. Tom Hill**
Author of Living At The Summit and co-author of Chicken Soup for the Entrepreneurial Soul

"The advice that is in the book is timeless. Get rid of debt, pay yourself first, and you will have paved the path to financial independence for yourself. When should you get started? There is no time like the present. How about now?"

- **Steve Johnson**
Author of the Bestselling Books If You are Not OutSelling, You're Being Outsold, and Selling Is Everyone's Business

"Unfortunately, I know from being in my industry that many Americans are losing "The Money Game." All of them should read this book. People have to understand the "rules" and develop the right habits as early as possible. This and only this will lead them to financial independence."

- **Michael Fleming**
CLU, Financial Services Representative

I would like dedicate this book to a number of different people, and it goes without saying to God, for all his guidance and wisdom, he has always shown me the way. First off to my parents Reggie and Clara Carden, who always taught me to have a vision and to go for whatever I wanted to achieve in life. The best piece of advice they gave was simply this. "You can do what you want to do, be what you want to be, and have what you want to have; this is the greatest country in the World, now go do something great with your life". Next to my sister Janella and my brother Alex who have always supported and pushed me to succeed. Also, to all my other family: grandparents, aunts, uncles, and cousins (especially JP) who also supported me through all my endeavors, and still do! To all my family I say thanks for the loving support!

To my wife Sarah, who has sacrificed more than imaginable, to help me live my dreams, and to her family for all the support and patience with me and my business. And finally to our new son Bryan... may you achieve everything in life you set out to accomplish!

There are a lot of others who have helped me along the way and I would like to list some of them below. To everyone on my list I say thank you and words can't express my gratitude for all the help.

Mark Norman
Steve and Elisa Johnson
Bob Davis
Adam Carroll
Michael St. Lawrence
The Bartick brothers G.A. and Paul
Matt Hawk
Bob Coakley
Adam Shavitz
Paul Lopez
Jack Litzelfelner
Tellee Warren
Zack Rhodes
Daryl Perkins
Carol Sealy
Matt Calinan
Nate Brooks
Mike Woods
Dr. Paul Schaffer
Mike Manual
Bill and Debbie Warren
The Barlow Family
Nick Thummel
Matt Moore

Thanks to all and best wishes!

Chad Carden

There have been two significant points in my life when my money future changed forever. The first was at the age of 20 when my dad told me, "Any money you receive from me from now on, consider it a loan." While it was as equally hard to hear as I'm sure it was to deliver, I knew from that point on if I was going to survive financially, it was up to me. Thanks for that, Dad.

The second important money memory I have was when my fiancee told me flat out she wouldn't marry my debt. I had to either get rid of it or she would get rid of me. Needless to say, with her help I buckled down and got rid of almost $6,000 in high interest debt in a matter of months. We've since lived our lives on the other side of the fence. I love you, Jenn, and all that you have done for me including putting my goals before your desires. I promise you I'll prove marrying me was the best decision you've ever made! You inspire me everyday to win the money game.

I'd like to thank the colleges and universities that have invited us in to deliver "The Money Game" to your students. Our goal has always been to change the way students look at money, and with your help, we will succeed. It takes someone of vision to bring in a new program that is critically important, but may or may not appeal to the masses. Your dedication to the students' well-being is what makes you great. Thank you for trusting our organization and what we stand for! I'd like to offer additional thanks to my brothers at Delta Sigma Pi who've continued to invite me in to their LEAD events to share my message with all of your students and alumni.

Thanks also to all the people who've offered words and acts of encouragement as Chad and I embarked on this wild ride of starting something great. You know who you are and are thought of often.

From the bottom of my heart...thanks.

Adam Carroll

What's Inside

Introduction

We get asked the same question all the time: What exactly *is* The Money Game? The simplest answer we can give is it's the game we all play with money everyday. It's based on the concept that at any given time in our lives we're either winning or losing the game, and unfortunately, more Americans (young and old) are losing. Our goal is to help change that! In today's world a lot of people are wondering, "What in the hell happened to my finances?" People have lost their 401K, are upside down in their house (their biggest "investment), can't find financing, and have lost their job. We cannot change the past, we can only affect and influence the future. We must focus on the future, and begin changing the way we think, and our habits surrounding money!

This book was written for young adults who are just getting started in their professional lives, but can be applied to nearly anyone in any financial situation. In the next several chapters, we'll take you through our own trials and tribulations, our own money mistakes, and the lessons we've learned along the way. We'll walk you through simple things you can be doing right now, no matter what your situation, that will help put you on the winner's path.

Congratulations, first of all, for taking the time to read a book on your personal finances! We have a hard time believing that something so important to success and happiness isn't taught in formal education. However, just reading the book isn't enough. We urge you to take the ideas and insights in this book and put them into practice. Chances are, you'll wish you'd started years ago.

Best of luck and enjoy the book!

Adam and Chad

Part One

Chapter One:

Money 101

"When I was young
I thought that money was
the most important thing
in life; now that I am old
I know that it is."

~Oscar Wilde

You are probably reading this book because you want to have more money. It goes without saying – we all do. It doesn't matter if you bought this book, someone gave it to you, or you just picked it up off the coffee table, you are reading it because you want more out of your finances. Notice we didn't say make more money, we said have more money. There is a big difference. In this book we will explore how you can continue to make the same amount of money and still keep more than ever before. We will help you set yourself up for success financially and actually win "The Money Game" (TMG).

Everyday we play TMG, and unfortunately a lot more people are losing the game than winning it. More than ever, it's critical that young and old alike understand what it takes (knowing the rules) of winning the game that we play with money. We are writing this book from our own experiences to give you what you need to be successful with this part of your life.

We believe becoming financially successful is simple, but not always easy. We are going to get real and keep this simple. Vince Lombardi always said it's the fundamentals that win games, keeping it simple and executing will prevail more times than not.

Why should you listen to us? First of all, we are not financial advisors. However, we have both done what it takes to go from losing to winning The Money Game. In addition, we've each presented to tens of thousands of students across the country who are all in a similar situation. We've discussed their challenges, their opportunities, and their plans to win the game for good. We're going to lay out the same information here.

Adam's Story

When I was growing up, I had no idea that my parents struggled financially. In fact, I was regarded in high school as one of the "wealthier" kids, an idea my Dad laughs at to this day. He's since confided in me that they occasionally put necessities on their credit cards just to get through the month. (You'd be amazed at how many parents have to do this!)

When I left home to go to college my parents had described in detail how they were going to help me pay for school. They would pay 100% of my expenses the first year, 75% the second, 50% the third and 25% the fourth year. Anything after four years was my own responsibility (which prompted me to get done in four!).

As most college students are, I was bombarded by credit card offers (most of them pre-approved) and finally gave in to the pressure and got one. Actually, I was hungry one day walking through the student union and someone was giving away a bag of peanut M&M's in exchange for filling out an application. The credit card was just a means to an end. Unfortunately, the end I had in mind cost me dearly.

By the time I was a junior in college, I had racked up almost $3,000 in credit card debt. To this day I can't tell you more than two or three things I purchased. Most of the debt came from dinners out, renting movies, buying clothes and shoes, and of course gas for my car. So looking back, virtually nothing I bought had any lasting value – dinners have come and gone (literally) before the credit card statement arrives, movies *have to be returned, clothes and shoes wear out, and gas is just a way to get from here to there.*

My last two years in college I piled another $3,000 in credit card debt on top of the original $3,000, making my grand total almost $6,000 by the time I graduated. Because I was paying for much of my schooling by this point, I had also managed to borrow about $23,000 in student loans. At one point I did the math and figured out that my portion of the tuition, room and board, and fees would've totaled about $12,000 for the last 3 years of school. Which begs the question: Where did that $11,000 go?

Lifestyle is the only answer I can come up with. I had my own apartment most of my senior year, which was ridiculous considering the fact that I was rarely there. My wardrobe came from the Gap, Eddie Bauer and J. Crew. I loved J.Crew clothing so much I felt compelled to order from the catalog every time I got one. (I think the folks at J.Crew knew that, considering the number of catalogs I got per year.)

There were two main influences driving my spending during college. The first was the fact that I was used to having nice things growing up in my parents' home. They were great to me, as I'm sure your parents are to you. The challenge this creates is a feeling of entitlement once we're out on our own. We forget that our parents struggled for forty years in order to be able to afford what they give us, and believe we deserve to immediately have everything we've become accustomed to. I assumed that because my parents could afford to order me clothes from J.Crew on a semi-regular basis, I could afford to do the same. I came across a saying that smacked me in the face just after college:

At some point in your life, you have to live like a college student. You'll either do it in college, or you'll do it as a professional. Entering my professional life, I was about to live like a college student.

*The second influence on my spending was my desire to keep up the image I had worked so hard at building. I was seen as successful by my friends even though I hadn't done anything particularly outstanding or impressive. I began to lump success and money in the same category – specifically, spending money I didn't have on things I didn't need. I was treating friends to dinners out or drinks at the bar, and justified it by keeping a mental tally of how much credit I had left on my cards. Yes, that's card**s**, plural. I was up to three by my senior year.*

When I graduated from college, I sold books door-to-door for a company based in Nashville, Tennessee. I did fairly well, making about $12,000 in 3 months. I wish I could tell you that's where my story got better. Unfortunately, the $12,000 was gone as fast as it came, most of it going to shoes, clothing and movies. I also took $5,000 of it and took a trip to Australia, New Zealand and Fiji for 3 months. Talk about a break from reality!

But something clicked in me around the age of 27 or 28 – I realized exactly what I wanted and how I was going to get it. And today at the age of 33, I have multiple businesses set up that pay me automatically on a monthly basis. I enjoy freedom and flexibility and am headed for a position of complete and total financial contentment while in my 30's.

Chad's Story

I remember when I was in college my thought process was something very similar to this: "When I get out of school I will make lots of money, pay off all my bills, and life will be good." Let me share with you what happened my first months after graduation. I left school and went to work for a large insurance company on a commission-only basis. As a matter of fact, I had to pay them rent to work out of their office. That lasted about a month, and they SENT ME a bill for $150 dollars. Then I sold cars at a well-known dealership in St. Louis, Missouri. I was working six days a week, on a commission basis that netted me about $250 a week or around $12,000 a year. My hours were 8AM to 8PM four days a week and the other two days were 8AM to 6PM (considered short days). I did that for three months and was living paycheck to paycheck every week. I was dating Sarah at the time, and she was giving me money to help me get by (Sarah was still in college at the time and I had the college degree).

After that I went to work for a labor service that gave you jobs daily and paid you daily. I would get up at 5AM, stand in line for a job, sometimes get one, sometimes not, and then after the day was over get a paycheck. It was an all-time low. I had about $60 dollars in my checking account, nothing in savings, $28,000 in debt and was borrowing money to pay rent. I remember the night that I hit bottom. I went to a job that they gave me and once I arrived was sent away because I was not a union member. I remember thinking, "How could they send me to a job, that I didn't qualify for....Why me?" I had exactly $58 dollars in my checking account, so I took $50 dollars out and headed off to the casino to make enough so I could pay my bills. 17 minutes later I had lost all $50 dollars, and headed home with $8 dollars to my name and still $28,000 in debt. I made a decision that night driving home that I was going to learn how to make, save, and invest money.

It has not been easy, and I have had to sacrifice a lot of things, but now ten years later I have built assets totaling over $1,000,000 at the age of 32. My money continues to grow and I now even make money when I am not working. I have set up multiple automatic investment accounts, and have enough money to have a little fun. I have since realized that life is much better on this side of the fence. You, too, can set yourself up for success if you put these principles to work. These principles are not new, and not hard to follow, but it will take some discipline. If you put into action what you read in this book, you can and will be on your way to winning "The Money Game."

So, as you can see, we've both been down the path of losing The Money Game. We want to share our stories so that others might not take the routes we took, and instead learn from the mistakes and head towards financial success. And if you find yourself having gone down that wrong path, we want to share with you ways to get back on track.

There are a couple things that are important to know before really diving into this book. These two concepts will help you understand the principles we talk about and give you an easier time putting things into action once you have read about them.

The first concept is that **time is on your side.** One of the advantages you have over anyone else is the amount of time you have to save and invest. Most people graduate and spend 5 to 10 years climbing out of the debt hole they have put themselves in, and then start to invest money somewhere around age 35-40. Why do people wait so long? It's simple: they don't have the extra money to invest. All of their money is being eaten up by bills, debt, and lifestyle. To take it one step further, a lot of people run out of money before they run out of month, every month. We will touch more on that later.

Most people want instant gratification. They want what they want, but are not willing to put forth effort or time. For example, which one would you rather have, $1 million or a penny that doubles everyday for a month? Let's explore what would happen with both choices. Obviously, with the $1 million you would simply have the million dollars. Now as for the penny that doubles, let's take a look:

Day 1	$.01	**Day 15**	$163.84
Day 2	$.02	**Day 16**	$327.68
Day 3	$.04	**Day 17**	$655.36
Day 4	$.08	**Day 18**	$1,310.72
Day 5	$.16	**Day 19**	$2,621.44
Day 6	$.32	**Day 20**	$5,242.88
Day 7	$.64	**Day 21**	$10,485.76
Day 8	$1.28	**Day 22**	$20,971.52
Day 9	$2.56	**Day 23**	$41,943.04
Day 10	$5.12	**Day 24**	$83,886.08
Day 11	$10.24	**Day 25**	$167,772.16
Day 12	$20.48	**Day 26**	$335,544.32
Day 13	$40.96	**Day 27**	$671,088.64
Day 14	$81.92	**Day 28**	$1,342,177.28

Are you changing your mind? This is only 28 days, which is February in a non-leap year! Most months have 30 or 31 days, and if you take it out to the 30 day mark you would have over $5.2 million dollars!! We live in a world where people want instant gratification. They want to have it all, but don't want to work for it, put in energy, or wait for it. People would rather have it now, when in the end they could have had so much more if they just exercised a little patience.

You may be asking, what is the point? The point is that even a small amount invested over time can grow into a huge amount – if you give it time – and time is exactly what you have. You might not have a lot of money, but you do have time. Keep this in mind as you read the following chapters and really focus on how time is your best friend, if you use it to your advantage.

"Empty pockets never held anyone back. Only empty heads and empty hearts can do that."

~ Norman Vincent Peale

The second concept is this: time can be your worst enemy if you let it take advantage of you. I know we just said that time is your best friend, so keep reading to understand what we mean. Most people want to live this year's lifestyle on next year's **if-come.** We in America call this credit. Don't get us wrong, credit is not all bad, but when used improperly, it can be your first step to losing TMG.

Consider these statistics:

- **92%** of all students have 1-2 credit cards by their sopho more year
- The average college student has a credit card balance around **$2,000,** or **$3,600** if paying for school with it (Overall average = **$2,800**)
- The average student loan debt for undergraduates is creeping up to around **$20,000**
- Unfortunately, it doesn't get any better after graduation: 40% of graduate students have credit card balances of **$6,000 or more**

"Some debts are fun when you are acquiring them, but none are fun when you set about retiring them."

~ Ogden Nash

- 15% of graduate students have credit card balances of **$15,000 or more**
- The average household credit card debt is over **$9,0000**
- **16.7** is the average number of credit cards per household

For your own information, here is a quick run down of how credit cards work: When you deposit money in a savings or money market account, your bank has the ability to loan out as much as 10 times that amount for things such as car loans, credit cards, and mortgages. Some banker had a great concept when they came up with this idea. You deposit a sum of money in savings and make 1% (if you're lucky!), and then borrow back $1,800 on a credit card and pay 19% interest. So basically what you are doing is borrowing your own money and paying it back at a high rate of interest. The banks are genius and we seem to be the not-so-smart ones. We are going to change that! We are going to show how to make interest work for you, not against you.

Looking at those statistics can be scary, and we know because we have lived it. A lot of people live their entire lives as a debt statistic and in the end LOSE The Money Game. We want you to bypass these stats and by doing so set yourself up for success financially. Keep in mind that it all starts when we are young. We can build the right habits, or fall victim to the wrong ones. The choice is up to us everyday!

In the following chapters we are going to uncover how to win TMG, and then it is up to you. We will give you all the tools to win, but it is you that has to put them into action, execute these principles, and most importantly, make them habits. We are going to cover:

Making, Saving, and Investing
Ongoing Savings
Needs vs. Wants
Essential Money Skills
Your Money Choices and Their Consequences

Are you ready? Good, let's get started!!

Key Points:

- Knowing the rules is the best way to win TMG.
- If you don't know the rules, chances are you are losing TMG.
- This whole book gives you the rules, but it is up to you to start taking action, changing your habits, and getting on the road to winning TMG!

Chapter Two:

Making, Saving, and Investing

"Every day
I get up and look through
the Forbes list of the richest people
in America. If I'm not there,
I go to work."

~Robert Orben

One of the biggest challenges we face is getting ahead financially, no matter how much we make. A wise man named Parkinson created a law that states that your expenses will rise to match your income. What does that mean? It simply means that if you make $30,000 a year, you will spend somewhere around $33,000 (most people spend about 10% more each year than they make). So, if you make $50,000 a year you will spend $55,000; likewise, if you make $100,000 a year you will spend $110,000. Why is that law so accurate? Because society, banks, and even you believe that if you make more you are entitled to more. Here is the change in thinking: *It is not how much you make, but how much of what you make you keep!* We think that is so important that we want to say it again. *It is not how much you make, but how much of what you make you keep!* We could tell you story after story about people who made $30,000 a year and retire with millions, and we can also tell you about people who make six figures and couldn't come up with $10,000 if they had to.

First, let's look at what you might expect to make after graduation.

The average college graduate makes roughly $30,000 their first year out of college. The top-paid career is engineering and they make, on average, around $52,000 a year. (Now don't go changing your major just yet). Is it possible that some graduates will make more than $52,000 a year their first year out? Absolutely! Is it realistic that most graduates will make less than $52,000 a year? Absolutely! We don't tell you this to scare you – keep in mind what we said earlier that it's not how much you make, but how much of what you make you keep!

Let's take three people and give them the same salary, $30,000 a year or $2500 a month. These three people have different personalities. One is a spender, one is an even-steven, and one is a saver. Let's take a look at what happens on a monthly basis.

The Spender $2,500	**The Even-Steven $2,500**	**The Saver $2,500**
Taxes $600	Taxes $600	Taxes $600
Apartment $600	Apartment $400	Apartment $0
Car $400	Car $300	Car $0
Insurance $100	Insurance $100	Insurance $100
Credit Card $200	Credit Card $100	Credit Card $100
Student Loan $300	Student Loan $200	Student Loan $200
Food $200	Food $200	Food $200
Miscellaneous $600	Miscellaneous $600	Miscellaneous $600
Leftover $-500	**Leftover $0**	**Leftover $700**

As you can see, the spender has higher payments for their apartment, their car, their credit card bill, and their student loan. The result of all these high payments is a negative $500 balance at the end of the month.

"Money is only a tool. It will take you wherever you wish, but it will not replace you as the driver."

~Ayn Rand

While the even-steven is spending less on their apartment and car, they are still living paycheck to paycheck (which, by the way, is how a lot of people live their whole lives).

The saver, meanwhile, is doing what is needed to win TMG – they are conserving money by living at home for a short while after graduation and saving the money they would normally pay as rent. They are also driving the same car they have had since high school until they can afford to put a substantial amount down on a newer car.

"There is no dignity quite so impressive, and no one independence quite so important, as living within your means."

~ Calvin Coolidge

Now who *looks* more successful? The spender does, of course, and this is an important concept to grasp. While the spender is living in a nice apartment, driving a nice car, and buying clothes on credit, what is happening to their financial reality? The spender looks like they are winning TMG, when in reality they are losing it big time. The saver, on the other hand, looks like they are losing TMG, when in reality; they are playing the game to win.

Later on we will revisit the saver and see exactly what happens with the extra money they have. Sometimes when it comes to looks, they can be deceiving. Some people have fancy things because they can afford them, but most people who have fancy things are scratching and clawing just to keep their head above water. The spender is $500 in the hole, and where do you think they go to cover everything? You guessed it...their credit card! So not only are they living beyond their income, they are also getting deeper in debt. Maybe it's time we redefine success!

The point we are trying to make is that whatever you earn, you must learn to live within, or even better, below your means. Then take the rest and invest it smartly and watch it grow. If you do this consistently, you will reach a point (sooner than you think) where your money works for you, you don't work for your money. When your money earns more money per month than you do in your job or business, you've created true financial freedom.

There's one main concept we want you to take from this chapter. If you're convinced that making more money is the answer to all your problems, you're dead wrong. It might help ease the strain a little, but you'll end up wanting more expensive toys with this new found "wealth." If you're focused on winning TMG, you should pay more attention to what you have left over at the end of the month. If you can increase that number and put that money to work for you (which we'll cover later), then you're on the track to winning.

Key points:

- It is not how much you make; it is how much of what you make you keep.
- Sometimes the people who look successful are actually losing TMG, and more importantly, those who look like they're losing may actually be winning!
- Never underestimate the power of the money you have left over at the end of the month and how it can actually go to work for you.

Chapter Three:

Ongoing Saving and Investing

"A bank is a place that will lend you money if you can prove that you don't need it."

~Bob Hope

Chad's Story

Before I became in tune with "The Money Game," every year on January 1st I would start what I thought was a savings account. Actually, it was a "put and take" account. You probably know how the story goes, put a little money in, and then take a little money out (sound familiar?). The cycle was endless, and my money was at a stand still. At the same time I had made some investments. People had always told me that I needed to invest in "blue chip" stocks. (A "blue chip" is the nickname for a stock that is thought to be safe, in excellent financial shape and firmly entrenched as a leader in its field. Blue chips generally pay dividends and are favorably regarded by investors. A few examples of blue chips are Wal-Mart, Coca-Cola, Gillette, Berkshire Hathaway and Exxon-Mobile.) So I invested in some "blue chip," but I also invested in some "green chip," some "red chip," some "white chip" and I had even invested in some "no chip stocks." I had also made some other investments. I had invested in things like JC Penney, Visa, MasterCard, and Discover. My "chip" investments were supposedly returning 5 . to 12% interest, while my "other investments" were costing me 18 to 24%, and once again I was at a stand still.

About five months after graduating from college I went to work for Mark Norman in St. Louis, Missouri. Mark owned the Dale Carnegie Franchise in St. Louis, and that is really where I learned to sell, speak, and do consulting. Mark taught me a lot, and one of the most important things he taught me was to pay myself first. When Mark told me to do this I was scared at first. I was deep in debt, and barely making enough money to pay my bills. Now he wanted me to take an extra 10% away and save it? I didn't think it was possible. But Mark promised me three things and all three were absolutely true. He said that I would never miss it (goes back to Parkinson's Law), that it would be there when I *needed it most, and probably the most important one, that I would be creating the right habit at an early age. Since then I have been paying myself first, and now I even save more than 10%.*

Most people know they should save and invest money, but they have no idea how to get started. In this chapter we are going to teach you the ins and outs of saving and investing your money. We will introduce the concept of "save/save" and other ideas you can put to use right away. When you read the next few pages, take a look in the mirror and ask yourself, "What do I need to do to make a positive step towards getting out of debt?"

The concept of "save/saving money": As most people save money, they don't really save it. They instead put a little bit away and then they take it right back out. *Save/saving* money means that when you put it away, it doesn't come out. Dollar cost averaging or automatic investment plans are the best way to "save/save" money.

Dollar cost averaging is a concept of buying into the stock market in intervals. You set aside an amount already determined every month or every quarter and you buy into mutual funds, stocks, etc. When you do this, the cost of the shares you buy over time will average out. You buy more shares when the market is low, and buy fewer shares when the market is high. This way of investing minimizes your risk and maximizes your return. Automatic investment plans work the same way. Every two weeks, month, or quarter, you set aside "X" amount of dollars that you put into some sort of savings account. Investing is not about investment performance, it is all about investor behavior. Creating the right habits now is the best thing

"Want to know someone's priorities? Just look at where they spend their money and their time."

~ Anonymous

you can do for your investments. Setting aside an amount will get you into the best habit of all: consistent investing!

Also, when you do this you allow your money to work hard for you, and you don't have to work so hard for your money. Take an acquaintance of ours named Andy. Andy has set himself up the right way from a very young age. He has multiple investments and earns interest on his invested money. To keep it simple, Andy makes money without working for it. He also did something early on that has helped him out greatly – he bought property investments. Andy owns three buildings for which he pays a total of $2700 a month (He has paid a few buildings off completely and owes $0 on those investments). Andy rents these buildings out to businesses and he collects $8700 a month. He has a gross profit of $6000 per month. Now, he has to pay maintenance and a property management company to help run everything, and that costs him 10%. So, Andy pays out an additional $800 a month, leaving him with a net profit of $5200. Andy doesn't work hard every month for the $5200, he works smart. We have to continue to find ways for our money to work hard for us. Working hard is great, if you are working smart at the same time!

The biggest reward on saving and investing is what Albert Einstein called "The 8th Wonder of the World," the power of compounding. The rule of 72 says that your money will double every 7 years when it grows at a rate of 10%. From the early 1900's until today, on average, the stock market has grown

10% a year. There have been ups and downs (the stock market crash of 1929 is one example, or what has been happening the past 18 months), yet overall the average growth rate on money is about 10% a year. This is also where time is in the favor of a young investor. Let's go back to our saver, and see where they would be at the age of 55?

> *"Understanding how to be a good investor makes you a better manager and vice versa."*
>
> ~ Charlie Munger

The SAVER had $700 left over, and let's assume that $200 of that is going somewhere else besides investments (clothes, food, lifestyle, etc.) So here is what it looks like:

Monthly investment: $500
Time Invested: 33 Years
Interest Earned: 10%
Total Invested: $198,000
TOTAL NEST EGG: $1,346,178

$1.3 million dollars might not seem like a lot of money to you, but if you have that much at 55, you are better off than 95% of other Americans at 55!

The point is ongoing saving and investing is a primary fundamental to winning TMG. Statistics say that most Americans save somewhere around 0%, and we have even seen some studies that say negative 7%! It begs the question, why aren't people saving more? The real reason may be they have no idea how to get started, or never got started in the first place. Now that you know, it's time to start saving!

Picture this: you walk into your bank one day and look at your account balances. (Whatever type of accounts you choose. We will talk about this in a later chapter). Your accounts add up to over $100,000. And you can do whatever you want with this money. How does it make you feel? In control? More secure? Open to new opportunities?

Having a sizable nest egg does a number of things to most people - it creates an openness to try new things, to do what you've always wanted to do, to invest in ideas that are appealing to you, to take vacations, to live with a freedom most people never experience. And the only way to get there is to begin to save/save now.

It's understandable to think this is a challenge. We relate it to working out – before a workout you might be saying to yourself, "I don't want to do this," but afterwards you never regret it. Just as you will never regret staying physically fit – you'll never regret saving money.

Key points:

- The key is not investment performance, it is ***investor behavior***. Build the right habits today.
- Don't just save money, save/save it.
- You will never regret saving money, and it will be there when you need it most.

Chapter Four:

Needs vs Wants

*"It's good to have money
and the things that money
can buy, but it's good, too,
to check up once in a while
and make sure that you haven't lost
the things that money can't buy."*

~George Horace Lorimer

This chapter alone can help find more ways to save money, not by making more, but by changing a few of your spending habits. This principle has changed our lives completely.

Study your spending habits and find out if there are a few places that you might be overspending. Let us save you some time – the answer is YES! Everyone spends money on things they don't need. Don't get us wrong, we are not saying to give up everything that is considered a want. What we are saying is don't sacrifice your needs or go deeply into debt, just to have what you want. Wait until you have some extra income (after you have paid all your bills, paid down your debt, and are save/saving money), to buy some of the extra things in life. We truly believe that you can have everything you want if you are patient and take care of the things you need to take care of first (pay your bills, pay off debt, and save/save money).

LendingTree came out with a genius commercial. It shows a man that has it all – a nice house, nice family, new cars, swimming pool, membership to the local country club, brand-new everything. Once you get the picture, the question is posed, "How do I do it?" His response? "I am in debt up to my eyeballs. I can barely afford to pay my finance charges." Unfortunately, this is common in America today. Most people will support this year's lifestyle on next year's if-come. Let us say that again. *Most people will support this year's lifestyle on next year's if-come.*

Most people will buy what they want, when they want, and have no concept of what it will truly cost them.

As we discuss essential needs vs. excessive wants, think about the things you have today. What things can you live without? Then after you cut those things out, what are you going to do with the money you have left over? Are you going to spend it foolishly on something else, or are you going to save/save it, and watch it grow? Once again the choice is totally up to you!

What are the essential things (needs) we all have to have in order to survive? Well, if you are in college you need tuition & fees, books, food (meal plan), housing, transportation, and clothing. If you are not in college, you need housing, transportation, clothing, and food.

After a speaking engagement last fall, we visited a college friend's apartment and found a big screen TV, a stereo that had to cost at least $500 (probably more), new furniture, and a very nice glass dining room table. Were all these things given to him? Having asked him, we can answer that out of a position of knowledge, NO!

He has two roommates, and all of them had to put these excessive wants on their credit card to "furnish" the apartment. They all had access to used furniture from their families, yet they "needed" new furniture. All of this to make their apartment look impressive.

This is where the blurry line comes in for most Americans; did they "need" it? Absolutely not, they just thought they needed it. Most people today think they have to have more things than they really need. So they end up overspending. We must change our mindset if we are going to change our habits. We want you to put down the book right now, and write down an inventory of what you possess. What things do you need and

*"Never keep up with the Joneses.
Drag them down to your level.
It's cheaper."*

~ Quentin Crisp

what things can you get rid of? Can you sell some things that might help you pay down your debt right now? After you take this inventory, the true test begins. What actions will you take in order to help your situation? The plan is great, but it is useless unless you take action.

Taking action involves deciding whether or not those excessive wants you now possess are helping or hindering your progress of winning TMG. As an example, if you've financed furniture or a television or *put clothes on a credit card* that isn't paid off, you have to ask yourself if you're sacrificing your financial future for excessive wants. Maybe you could try doing something similar to the story that follows...

Adam's Story

A good friend of mine in college had a fetish for Air Jordan shoes and CDs. By the time we graduated, he had 25 pairs of Air Jordan's dating back to the time he was in junior high school, and a collection of over 600 CDs. By the time he was in his mid-twenties he realized how foolish he'd been. His credit card balance was nearing $7,000 and the minimum payments were barely covering his interest charges every month. Instead of burying his head in the sand and doing nothing about it, he got *proactive. He sorted his CD collection into A, B, and C stacks. The A stack he listened to regularly. All of the B's and C's he took to a CD reseller. The 400 CDs he sold generated him about $1,200 to pay down debt. He tackled the shoe collection next. After finding someone that would sell merchandise for him on E-bay, my friend was able to unload 18 pairs of Air Jordan's for a total of $2,600. Some of the earlier styles went for as much as $225 each! By getting creative and proactive about his debt, he was able to knock out $3,800 of his $7,000 balance.*

With the popularity of sites like Craigslist and Ebay, it's easier than ever to sell the stuff that clutters up your apartment or parent's house. The items you no longer need or want are what we call lazy assets. Things that have bogged down your ability to save money and/or pay off debt. You'll want to take the inventory list of all the unwanted items and begin to use the cash from those lazy assets to get back on the path to winning TMG.

We want you to understand one thing - everyone has excessive wants. These wants aren't necessarily bad if you take care of all your needs first, pay off your debt, and save/save money. If you are doing all these things, then we say go out and enjoy yourself. But if you are caught in the overspending game, and most of it is on your credit card, the things you're buying will make you feel horrible when you know you've sacrificed your financial future for them. It's amazing how much enjoyment you can get out of excessive wants when you know you paid cash for them. Alter your thinking about your needs and wants and you'll be on your way to WINNING The Money Game!

Key points:

- Eliminated wants now will help you get them in the future at no extra cost.
- Don't spend need money on wants; you just dig yourself into a deeper hole.
- If you discipline yourself you can have more of the things you want than you have ever imagined.

Chapter Five:

Essential Money Skills

"In the old days
a man who saved
money was a miser;
nowadays he's a wonder."

~Author Unknown

How does interest work? What bank accounts should I have? How do I eliminate unnecessary fees? We get these questions and many more when we put on programs across the country. We are going to take you through the essential money skills you need in order the win TMG. Some of this stuff may seem like common sense. Please be patient, and have an open mind. Remember, it is not what you know, but your actions that determine results.

We are going to break down six skills that you need (balancing a checkbook, using a monthly budget, limiting impulse buys, having the proper accounts, eliminating unnecessary fees, and understanding interest). As we go through each one, think about your level of knowledge with each skill. Evaluate where you are, and what you need to do to learn more about the skills you lack. We are going to give you everything you need in its simplest form, and keep in mind that learning is a process. Let's get started!

• Balancing a Checkbook

It's fairly obvious that one of the keys to winning TMG is knowing how much money you have in the first place. Because most people keep the majority of their money in their checking account, that's where we'll start. And we'll start with a story of what NOT to do.

Adam's Story

The bank I used in college allowed me unlimited ATM usage each month. From the ATM I could do withdrawals, deposits, and balance transfers. To set the record straight, I was horrible at balancing my checkbook. I'd put multiple things on my debit card and forget to record the transaction in my checkbook – does this sound familiar?

Being the creative, intelligent college student that I was, I figured out a way to keep myself from getting hit with overdraft charges (Insufficient Funds Fees or NSF fees). Or so I thought. Every time I'd go out and write a check or use my debit card on something, I'd round up to the nearest $5 and transfer that amount from my savings to checking. It works great until you forget to transfer the money a couple (okay, 6) times. In one month my bank charged me $180 in overdraft fees because I'd forgotten to transfer money from savings to checking. All 6 checks I wrote bounced at the bank and 2 of them were to places that charged me an additional $25 for accepting a bounced check. All together, my fool-proof checkbook balancing act cost me $230 in one month!

I've since changed my ways. Today, every time I spend anything on my debit card or write a check, it immediately goes in the checkbook. If I don't have access to the checkbook right away, I've identified a small box where those receipts go as soon as I get home. When I balance my checkbook, I check the box to see if I've missed any receipts.

"A bank book makes good reading - better than some novels."

~Harry Lauder

You should also reconcile your checkbook when you get your bank statement every month, or as you use online banking you should look at your accounts twice per month. Reconciling is a big word for going through your bank statement, either online or when you receive it in the mail, and making sure all of the checks you wrote or debits you made have cleared. It also forces you to make sure your balance and the bank's balance on your account match. Banks screw up too sometimes, so it's a good idea to get in the habit of reconciling.

With free online tools like www.mint.com and www.yodlee.com it's easier than ever to keep an up-to-date view on your bank account. These services have text messaging features and alerts that will tell you when checks clear, payments are due, and when you've gone over your budget which we'll cover next.

• Using a Monthly Budget

Using a monthly budget is critical to finding what we call your "N." We borrowed "N" from a financial guru Nick Murray. (Thanks Nick.) The 'N' we are talking about is the amount of money you have left-over at the end of the month (or for some, your "N" might be negative....This is not good!)

The key to a monthly budget is keeping it simple. What is your income after taxes? What are your fixed expenses? (Expenses that don't change like rent, car payment, etc.) What are your flexible expenses? (Expenses that vary from month to month like phone bill, utilities, etc.) And finally, what are your extras? Again we suggest that you use the following sample budget and figure out what your 'N" is right now.

SAMPLE BUDGET SHEET

Income Amt Per Month	
Money from Family	
Savings	
Part-Time Work	
Financial Aid	
TOTAL INCOME	
Fixed Expenses	
University Registration Fees	
School Books & Supplies	
Dorm Room & Board or Rent	
Auto Insurance	
Health Insurance & Prescriptions	
Student Loan Payments	
Flexible Expenses*	
*Your personal choices affect these expenses	
Groceries	
Utilities & Telephone Bills	
Car Payments	
Gas & Car Maintenance	
Public Transportation	
Credit Card Payments	
Toiletries	
Clothing & Laundry	
Social/Recreational Activities	
Club Dues	
Extras	
Eating Out	
Cable TV	
Books & Magazines	
Gifts	
Vacations	
TOTAL EXPENSES	

TOTAL INCOME-TOTAL EXPENSES= "N"
(Should not be a negative number)

After you figure out your "N," or how much money you have left over, you can then find ways to increase your "N", by cutting out flexible expenses and cutting corners on your excessive wants. After you do this, it is time to figure out what to do with your extra money. We suggest you save/save it! (Surprise, Surprise.) Once again, this is up to you. This will take some action on your part, but if you do it now and create the right habits, it becomes easier as you get older. Knowing if you are winning or losing TMG is one of the most important things you can do!

- **Limiting Impulse Buys**

Chad's Story

When I was a freshman in college my roommate wanted to get a brand-new car. He was already driving a newer truck, and by all means it was a nice vehicle for a college freshman. He asked me to go down to the dealership with him and look for cars. When we were looking he found a sports car that was a year old with 9500 miles on it. It was a very nice car, and a little out of his price range. He had some extra student loan money that he could use as a down payment that would allow him to be able to afford the monthly payments and get approved for a loan. He made a down payment of $3500 (student loan money) and had a payment of $318 every month.

Let's fast forward and look at his situation as a college sophomore. One year later, he was two months behind on his payment and had his parents bail him out. Now that $3500 he used as a down payment let's see what it truly cost him? His student loan interest rate is 6% and he is paying it off in ten years. That is an extra $2800 dollars he is paying on that down payment, bringing it to a total of $6300 (which he is still paying on today). I spoke with him about it for this book, and *he is still kicking himself for making that purchase. We talked about how he might not have made the decision to buy the car, if he would have thought the situation through. Why did he make that mistake? Because he made an impulse decision which led to a bad impulse buy!*

Have you ever bought something on impulse? The answer for 99.9% of us is yes. Most impulse buys turn out to haunt us as a bad decision we made. We usually feel some sort of guilt, and wish we could go back and think the situation through. Impulse buying happens when we are not prepared. If we were prepared, we would know exactly what we are buying and not buying each trip to the store, mall, car dealership, furniture store, real-estate office, etc. Cutting down on impulse buying can be a great way to increase your "N." For example, when you go shopping for clothes, make sure you know what you are looking for, buy it, and get out. What if you don't know what you are looking for? Then, even better, have a limit on what you are going to spend, and don't go over it!

- **Having the Proper Accounts**

Chad's Story

I sold cars in the summer and on Saturdays when I was in college to make some extra money and improve my skills in dealing with people. After you sell a car, most people will fill out a credit application, get approved or denied, and the process moves from there. Once someone is approved, they then move into the Finance and Insurance office (F&I), and deal with the F&I Manager. I had a chance to work closely with my F&I manager, and Willie taught me a lot about the business. One thing he taught me was that, for some reason, creditors will look closely at what type of bank accounts you have or don't have. For example, you are more likely to get approved (all other things being equal) if you have both a checking account and savings account. One or the other by itself is not as good. Not having any accounts at all hurts your chances even more. You would be amazed how many people don't have the proper accounts. As we travel the country we find more and more people not having the right accounts, if they have any accounts at all.

One time when I was on vacation a buddy of mine asked me to take his ATM card and get some money out for him since I was headed that way. I told him, "no problem!" When I grabbed the receipt from the ATM I noticed that he had over $30,000 sitting in his checking account. $30,000 in your checking account is absurd! You are not making any interest on that money, and with inflation it's actually costing you money. That money should be in a money market account, or at the very least, a savings account. I realized right then that a lot of people don't understand what type of accounts they should have. So we are going to go through them. If you don't have your money in the proper accounts, then take action now! You could be losing money!

"The only reason many American families don't own an elephant is that they have never been offered an elephant for a dollar down and easy weekly payments."

~Mad Magazine

Checking Account: Checking accounts should be used to pay bills and have a little left over for spending. You should not keep any more than five hundred dollars in your checking account after all your monthly bills are paid. Why? Because in a checking account your money does not gain interest or make you any money. There is no need to have more than that. If you do, you are actually costing yourself money. Also, if you have it in your checking account it is easier to spend. Subconsciously you will begin to make it easier on yourself to spend this money, because it is readily available. Use your checking account to pay bills, and leave a little left over for spending.

"Always borrow money from a pessimist, he doesn't expect to be paid back."

~Author Unknown

Savings Account: Use your savings account as your "rainy day fund." Begin by setting up an automatic deduction from your checking account into your savings account. As the balance keeps growing, remember this money is to be used for emergencies only! You'll want to keep anywhere from $500 to $2,000 there in case of emergency. This money is liquid, which means you can get to it without penalty. You should make it hard on yourself to use this money unless you absolutely need to. Also, in a savings account you will gain interest or make money on the money you have in the account. It will be a very small percentage, but at least you are gaining something!

Money Market: Money Markets are similar to savings accounts; however, they usually have a higher interest rate or rate of return. Typically, a money market account requires that you carry a minimum balance of $1,000, so when your savings account grows to that level, consider transferring money to the account paying higher interest. Money Markets are also liquid, so there would be no penalties if you needed this money. Using a money market would be good for a need within a 1-2 year time frame, such as a down payment on a car, house, condominium, or if you need it to pay off a student loan as soon as you graduate.

CD: A CD or a "Certificate of Deposit" is an account which is not liquid, meaning you have to keep your money in there for a certain amount of time before you have access to it without penalty. CDs are good for longer investments of 3-5 years. You will have a higher rate of return on it (higher interest rate). Only buy CDs with money you won't "need" anytime soon. You should plan on putting money in a CD that you can leave there and invest for a longer term. For example, if you know that in 3-5 years you want to buy a house, your down-payment money will make you more in a CD than in a savings account. CDs are great for investments with a little longer time period!

- **Eliminating Unnecessary Fees**

In the past few years, banks have begun to make a majority of their income from usage fees, penalties, and other access fees that are charged to their customers. Most of the fees that are charged by banks are entirely avoidable, however BILLIONS of dollars are made every year from these fees simply because consumers aren't paying attention.

There are plenty of people who think that if there are checks in the checkbook then they have money. Additionally, with the increased use of debit cards, it's even easier to spend money you don't have. NSF fees or Insufficient Funds fees are a huge source of revenue of banks all across the country. So, wouldn't it go without saying that balancing your checkbook and knowing what you actually have in your account would be a great way to eliminate these fees? We think so too.

One thing you can do is get overdraft protection from your bank. This is a service your bank provides that will automatically transfer money from your savings to your checking account should you write more checks than you have money for in checking. Another great reason to have a savings account!

One other junk fee that banks will charge is an ATM usage fee for utilizing an ATM machine at another bank. Consider switching your accounts to a bank that won't charge you if you have to use an ATM machine, or will rebate the added fee back to your account each month. Pay close attention to your monthly statement. Some banks are even charging their customers if they go over a certain number of debit transactions each month. It may be wiser to run the transaction as credit instead of debit when you swipe your debit card. Each bank varies on how they handle this.

Many "rewards" credit cards charge an annual fee in order to even carry the card. If you have an annual fee do one of two things: Either call your credit card company to waive the fee or get rid of that card and get one that does not have an annual fee. Most cards that have annual fees have extra "perks" with them; the problem is a lot of people don't use the "perks," thereby wasting money.

"Beware of little expenses; a small leak will sink a great ship"

~ Benjamin Franklin

Your credit card company will also charge you extra interest or a late fee if you are late making a payment. Make sure you pay your credit cards on time! That goes for all bills. Again, with the free online services available, it's easier than ever to set up automatic reminders or automatic payments that will eliminate late fees and penalties.

"He who does not economize will have to agonize."

~ Confuscious

The question we are always asking is: why pay fees you don't have to? If you are winning TMG, you have a "rainy day" fund, a budget for yourself, and you are disciplined enough to hold yourself accountable, you don't have to worry about these fees. Quit making the banks and lenders more money, and put it back into your pocket.

One of the most common reasons that we find people in financial hardship is because they are aren't paying attention to the additional fees that are being charged to them. Winning The Money Game is simple – pay close attention to where your money is going and eliminate the fees where you can.

- **Understanding Interest**

Interest, like time, can be your best friend or worst enemy. If you are paying interest it can become your worst enemy and if interest is being paid to you, then it is your best friend. Interest can be very complicated, but we are going to keep it simple. Here is a golden rule when it comes to interest and winning TMG, ***Do Your Homework!*** If you borrow money – for a car, house, personal loan, or whatever else, you must figure out the total cost of the loan. Most people look only at their monthly payment. The question you have to ask yourself is how much interest am I being charged and what will it cost me in the end? Get the lowest interest rate possible by shopping around – don't settle on the first loan you see.

> *"People are living longer than ever before, a phenomenon undoubtedly made necessary by the 30-year mortgage."*
>
> ~Doug Larson

You've no doubt heard about the sub-prime mortgage meltdown that caused so many problems in the real estate industry (and eventually brought down some of the largest and most well-known investment banks!). One of the underlying causes of the unraveling of the financial sector was the fact that so many consumers got adjustable rate mortgages (ARMs). There was a significant lack of education when these individuals and couples got their mortgages, many of whom had no idea what the real effect of their interest rate going up at least a point and in some cases multiple points was going to be. In the end, a vast majority of these homes that had adjustable rate mortgages were foreclosed on as the homeowners couldn't afford the new payments. The foreclosures created a gigantic problem with home values across the country and eventually caused the housing bubble to burst and home prices to plummet.

It wouldn't be safe to assume that none of this would've happened if consumers had ultimately been educated about the effect that the interest would eventually play. It is safe to say that a greater number of homeowners would've either kept their homes or not bought them in the first place. Either way, you can prevent a mistake of this kind by understanding the choices and options you have when you finance a house, a car, or anything else for that matter. The key is asking around, doing your research, and knowing your options before making a decision.

Now on the opposite side of the fence, if you are **earning** interest, you are beginning to understand how to win the game we all play with money. Just as you pay interest to the credit card companies, the mortgage company, the car financing company, you can also loan money out or invest it and earn interest (sometimes with great rates of return).

The simplest ways to earn interest on your money would be to invest in a CD (Certificate of Deposit), a money market account, a savings bond, or a municipal bond. There are other options but are a little more involved and require additional information and education before investing. These include investing in second mortgages, tax lien certificates, and making small business micro loans.

Tax lien certificates are purchased by investors when someone fails to pay the property taxes on their home or business. The investors can make up to 24% per year in some states and may end up owning the property for what they have invested in property taxes. This kind of investing is usually done by very savvy investors who have a fairly sizable amount of money to invest. The beauty of these investments is there is relatively little risk and a huge upside reward.

In your lifetime, the interest you pay on your debt will be one of your two greatest expenses. The interest you earn, however, could account for a great portion of your future wealth. So the choice is yours. You can either pay more than your fair share of interest, or earn more than your fair share of interest. Which will you choose and how will you change your ways to make sure you know you're paying the least and earning the most?

Key points:

- Knowing the essential money skills is one of the easiest ways to win TMG.
- Using a budget is key to making sure you are getting ahead and not digging a deeper hole.
- Interest will either work for you or against you, the key is it's up to you.
- Taking action to understand the rules is your responsibility; take action today!!!

Chapter Six:

Your Money Choices and Their Consequences

"The safe way to double your money is to fold it over once and put it in your pocket."

~Frank Hubbard

This chapter will be an eye-opener for most people. It was for us, once we truly understood that we had to pay back everything we borrowed. The eye-opener was just how much we had to pay back. It was a lot more than the amount we borrowed, that's for sure!

For example: It will take 18 years to pay off a credit card with a balance of $2500 if you only pay the monthly minimum. Can you imagine paying off $2500 over 18 years? The scary thing is that a lot of people are doing it right now! Houses get paid off quicker than some credit card debts. We could bore you with statistics, instead, let's use some examples to really figure this out. We are going to start with student loans. If you don't have student loans or won't ever get student loans, feel free to skip this part and move on to the next example. We'll cover credit cards next. If you don't have credit card debt, give yourself a big pat on the back, but still read this because we don't want you to fall to the mercy of it down the road!

- **Student loans**

Student loans are not a bad thing. In fact, they are instrumental in helping people get a higher education. If they are used correctly, they have priceless value. The challenge is that most of the time student loans are used for more than they are intended. Lenders today make it easy for you to have access to extra funds. When you get a student loan refund check, it seems like "free money," and you don't think about the fact you have to pay it back. We would have, on average, an extra $1,500 a semester, and would use every penny on things that had nothing to do with college classes, books, or fees. This is where you get into trouble. After graduation, you may realize (like we did) that you have an extra $12,000 to pay back, and not one dime of it went to higher education. Let's take a look at two students and see how they used their student loans, but more importantly what consequences they faced because of their choices and actions.

"By the time I have money to burn, my fire will have burnt out."

~ Author Unknown

John and Sam both went to the same college at the same time. It took them both four years to graduate and both of them had to use student loans to help pay for school. Because their parents were economically equal they both received the same amount of student loans to get their degrees. It cost each of them $15,000 in student loans to make it through all four years. Sam, however, borrowed $10,000 more for miscellaneous things, such as spring break, nights out, and fraternity dues. John had the same amount of fun in college, but he worked a part-time job to fund his extra-curricular activities. So when they graduated, John had $15,000 in student loans and Sam had $25,000 in student loans. They each had a 6% fixed interest rate, and paid $170 dollars a month to pay off their loans. How long did it take John to pay it off? Ten years, and he actually paid $20,400 on his borrowed $15,000. Not a bad thing since John did need his loan to get his degree. Now, it took Sam 20 years to pay his off, and he actually paid $40,800 for his borrowed $25,000. They both had the same monthly payment, and it took Sam an extra 10 years and roughly $20,000 more because of the choices he made in college.

"Ben Franklin may have discovered electricity, but it is the man who invented the meter who made the money."

~ Earl Warren

Please understand, we are not saying don't have fun in college. As a matter of fact, we encourage you to have as much fun as possible. College is the best time of your life and it should be enjoyed. However, you don't want to leverage your future fun for today's fun. Every dollar you borrow today for fun is a dollar of fun you won't be able to have after you graduate.

Some of the savviest students we've spoken to are doing things totally creatively to fund their fun in college. Here are a few examples:

Tim set up a website company and doesn't know how to program websites! He uses online resources like 99designs.com and rentacoder.com to outsource the building of websites. He charges $4-5,000 on average and it usually costs him around a thousand to have the site built by freelancers. His goal is to have a project a month.

Amanda advertised her tutoring services on Craigslist and is charging $45 an hour to tutor kids in Math and Spanish. Satisfied parents are her greatest source of referrals and are HAPPY to pay her the $45. Sure beats answering phones for $7 an hour.

Ryan bought a used lawn mower his freshman year and started a mowing company that now has 3 trucks, 4 teams of mowers, and an annual revenue of almost $800,000. He's 23, recently graduated (with no debt), and has the world at his feet.

If student loans are a necessity for you, then by all means, use them. It's what they're there for. However, when you're figuring out what you'll need for school, keep in mind the notion of not leveraging future fun. If you think you can have fun on borrowed money, the amount of fun you can have when you're paying cash will blow your mind. Trust us, we know.

- **Credit Cards**

Credit cards, like student loans, are not a bad thing. As a matter a fact, we can make an argument that every college student needs a credit card for emergencies, to help build their credit, and to create the right habits. The challenge is most students don't just use it for emergencies and wind up hurting their credit and building the wrong habits. Let's take a look at two different students and how they managed, or mismanaged, their credit.

Throughout college, Jennifer had to use her credit card for some emergencies (like auto repair and books) and when she graduated she had a balance of $1,500. Sarah used her credit card for emergencies too, but also for shoes, nights on the town, and Spring Break, and her balance when she graduated was $3,800. When they graduated, they both went to work and they both were making $30,000, which was just enough to survive with their apartment and other bills.

They both were paying the minimum payment each month of $30. Jennifer will pay off her balance in 8 years if she continues to pay the minimum balance. She will pay a total of $3,000, which is an extra $1,500 in interest. In Jennifer's case, she paid exactly double what she borrowed.

Now with Sarah, it will take her 50 years to pay off her credit card if she continues to pay the minimum. **50 YEARS!** She will pay a total of $18,000 which is an extra $14,200 in interest. And all for what - shoes, and a little bit of extra fun? Once again, we are not saying that Sarah shouldn't have gone on Spring Break and bought the shoes she wanted. We are saying that she should have found an alternative way to pay for them besides her credit card. Ultimately, she was funding her shoes and trips with if-come. Only, if-come didn't come fast enough.

The point is, use your credit cards wisely. Don't get behind the financial eight ball and dig yourself a deeper hole like Sarah did. Build the right habits, not the wrong ones. Focus on paying more than the minimum every month if you can't afford to pay it off in full. If you can eat it, drink it, or wear it, always pay cash. If you already have bad habits when it comes to spending, work like hell to break them. You will never regret it!

What does all of this mean? Every choice we make has a consequence, some good, some bad, some immediate and some delayed, but EVERY choice we make has consequences, and when it comes to money, they are not forgiving.

Take a look in the mirror. What choices are you making right now? Are you borrowing money to fund fun? Will you like the consequences? Will your future lifestyle be effected by what you're doing today? What changes do you need to make?

It all goes back to what we said in Chapter One. What will you do to change your situation? What actions will you take? What habits will you build, or more importantly, what habits will you break to win "The Money Game?"

Key points:

- Use credit wisely or it will cost you big in the end.
- The choices you make today have consequences–some good and some bad. Choose Wisely.
- Changing your money habits now will help improve your financial future; take action today.

Part Two

In Part Two we are going to give you the "how to's" and tools you need to really make a change. We are going to walk you through a plan on where to start, keep track of progress, and see positive results. This part will give you everything you need to put all these theories into action. The question again is, will you? By now you should have a budget for yourself, you should know your needs, and you should have an idea of where your "N" is. Now is when the fun begins!

As the title of this book suggests, we all play a game with money. At any given point in our lives we're either winning the game or losing it. We want you to WIN! So, we've broken Part 2 into four chapters that spell GAME. By following our "rules" of winning, you'll begin to see noticeable improvements in your financial well-being. The first steps are difficult, but just like with exercise, you'll never regret taking the first steps once you've finished this financial workout!

The Rules are:
Grow With Your Money
Assets Vs. Liabilities
Monitor Your Progress
Evaluate Your Progress

Chapter Seven:

Grow With Your Money

"Money isn't the most important thing in life, but it's reasonably close to oxygen on the "gotta have it" scale."

~Zig Ziglar

Most college students take general education classes their first couple of years to "get their feet wet" in college and try to determine what major they'll pursue. What's amazing to us is the fact that you'll spend $10-20,000 on studying things like humanities (which you won't use again), astronomy (which is basically a class on impressing your dates), and Sociology (a class created to show us how different we all are) yet most people aren't willing to spend 10-20 bucks and a weekend reading a book on their finances. In fact, it's said that the average college graduate reads .9 books a year. You read that right - not even a complete book.

The point of this chapter is simple: you have to grow (i.e. educate yourself) financially if you ever want to win The Money Game. We're assuming that one of the reasons you went to college was to get a good degree and as a result, get a good job. Because with a good job comes a good salary, right? The challenge with this logic is if your financial ability hasn't grown, that big salary will be gone before you know it.

The great business philosopher Jim Rohn says, "Look in any half-million dollar home and you'll find a library. They didn't buy the library once they built the home, rather they were able to build the half-million dollar home because of the library." Sure, some of the books will be fiction, some mystery novels, but you can be sure that a great percentage of the books will have something to do with wealth generation.

As you enhance your knowledge and skills in certain areas during college, be sure and grow in financial education as well. It's not enough these days to be a great teacher, great psychologist, great web developer, you must also be a great money manager, be great with a budget, and a dedicated investor.

*"Experience is a good school,
but the fees are high."*

~ Heinrich Heine

There's a philosophy that we buy into that says if you are not a good steward of your money, you will have a difficult time getting any more of it. Another way to look at it is money begets money. It's amazing how quickly your total balance will grow when you are dedicated to saving a percentage of your income every month. New opportunities will arise that you hadn't seen before and yet you'll start to want less because you have more in your bank account. It's a difficult concept to grasp, but an amazing feeling once you've achieved it.

Adam's Story

About four years out of college, my wife (then-girlfriend) and I got very serious about paying down our debt and putting ourselves in a position to win The Money Game. We bought a condo in Denver, Colorado, and had started a nice financial safety net in a money market account. It was awesome to see the balance grow every month towards our goal of having $20,000 in the account. There was the occasional blip downward if one of the cars broke down, but we knew we'd be back on track the next month. It took us close to two years to hit the $20,000 mark, and during that time we'd paid cash for everything.

A strange thing happened to me during that two year time period and it's stuck around ever since. I've always wanted a big screen TV. When HDTV came out, I wanted one. When plasma TVs came out, I wanted one. And we certainly had enough money in the account to buy any television we wanted. But along the way, the desire to have a nice TV got smaller than the desire to build real wealth.

I read a book called The Cashflow Quadrant by Robert Kiyosaki that changed the way I looked at money and spending. In the CQ, Kiyosaki talks about putting your money to work for you in real estate and other investments. He tells the story of wanting a Porsche and his mentor telling him he can either spend thousands of dollars on a Porsche, or he can go out and spend the same amount on a down-payment on real estate that would end up making the Porsche payment. In the end, the second option would give him a cash producing asset (the real-estate) and a pretty nice car to drive around. ***This is what it means to grow with your money****. It's about getting smarter with the money you have so that you don't have to work your tail off for the next 40 years to retire on 1/3 of what you couldn't get by on in the first place.*

There are two keys to growing with your money and they are reading books on wealth creation and finding a mentor who's already been there and succeeded. Between the two of us we've read over 400 books on money management, wealth building, business, and real estate. We've also reached out to professionals and financially savvy investors to learn from their successes and failures. It's absolutely amazing what someone else can teach you that's already been through the trials. They'll literally shave years off your learning curve and get you to financial success that much sooner!

We'll finish the chapter with this thought: Growing with your money is essential to achieving lasting financial success. You have to grow your skills, your knowledge, your understanding, your ability to delay gratification and most importantly, your ability to see the bigger picture of what your money can do for you.

Key points:

- Make it a goal to read (at the very least) one book on your finances this year, in addition to this one!
- It's not enough just to be good at what you do. You must understand your finances.
- You'll be amazed how money begets money. If you don't start saving, it won't have a chance to grow.

Chapter Eight:

Assets vs. Liabilities

"It's good to have money and the things that money can buy, but it's good, too, to check up once in a while and make sure that you haven't lost the things that money can't buy."

~George Horace Lorimer

To make this chapter fairly simple to understand, we want to make distinctions about assets and liabilities. An asset is something that puts money in your pocket. A liability is something that takes money out of your pocket.

Using these definitions, what most people think are assets (cars and homes), are really liabilities. After all, every month you have to make a car payment, right? Every month you have to make a mortgage payment, right? Now, for people who own their cars outright, it's a different story as far as monthly payments, but they still own liabilities. A car can break down, a house might need major repairs. Unless you are deriving money from owning these things, cars and homes are liabilities, not assets.

This was a hard pill for us to swallow right after college. Let's face it, every new college grad wants a new car (or at least a newer car). And some of us will go to any length to get something that we are proud to drive around. Here are our car stories:

Adam's Story

When I started my sophomore year in college, my mom and dad gave me $3,000 to pick out a car. After hours of searching (4 hours!) I found what became affectionately known as Air Force One. A 1987 Buick Somerset. What sold me on the car was the fact that it was two-door, had a 5-speed manual transmission, and had a completely digital dashboard and radio. This beast was state-of-the-art for a 1987 hoopty. With a mere 114,000 miles on the odometer, I thought I had found a gem.

Air Force One lasted through college and about a year beyond until I had a job selling radio advertising and was embarrassed to be seen in it.

A successful salesperson wouldn't be seen in a car like that! (Or so I thought.) When I decided to look for a newer car, the dealership told me that my trusty Somerset was worth a whopping $100. Once I mustered all the pride I had left inside I took the Benjamin they were offering and traded in my car for a 1995 Ford Contour. The kicker for me was the sunroof and leather seats. To say it was an ugly car would be an understatement.

At this point in my life I thought I was pretty savvy when it came to making decisions like buying a car. Little did I know that the salesman would take my head off at the financing table. (When you decide to buy your first car, make sure to take your parents with you.)

I drove the Ford Contour for about 2 years until my father-in-law told me the transmission was going out on it. When I traded it in on a 2001 Honda Civic for my wife, I was about $3,000 upside down on the Contour (meaning I owed more than it was worth.)

There were great lessons I learned from my mistakes in the car buying world. First and foremost, I always know what a car is worth before I decide to buy it. Secondly, I've since arranged my own financing through a bank or credit union where they're not out to screw you (completely). And lastly, my wife and I realized early on that having car payments every month was not a way to get us where we wanted to be financially. So, we've accelerated the payments on every car we've had since to pay them off within a year or so. Today, my wife and I both drive 4-5 year old cars that are in great shape, need few repairs, and are paid off in full.

Chad's Story

I was very fortunate my parents "helped" me with my first few cars. In 1998, it was time to buy my first car. I was driving a 1993 Ford Probe, which was a nice car, with not too many miles on it. I could have driven it for two or three more years, but I NEEDED a new car. So I went out and traded my probe for a 1996 Chevy Camaro. It was red and looked sharp. It was much more car than I really needed, but nonetheless, it was mine (actually it was the bank's car!). I financed it for 60 months (normal for an auto loan) and left the finance office with 13% interest. 13% was not very good, considering used car interest rates were running 6-8% on average. I ended up paying way too much for the car, and had a much higher interest rate than I should have. Why? Because I had no idea what I was doing. I later went on to sell cars, and witnessed 95% of the people that came through the door had little or no knowledge on the process of buying a car.

I learned a lot buying that car and learned even more when I sold them. You must do your homework before buying a car. Not only finding out the value of the car, but also the going interest rates, and if you need to buy extended warranties or not. Knowledge is definitely power when buying a car, and the more you know the better off you will be.

When we talk about assets and liabilities, it may seem somewhat impossible to generate money from assets while you're in college. If real estate is something that appeals to you and you are a fairly handy person when it comes to home repair, consider buying a home to rent to your friends in college. It's something we wish we had done in school, but didn't have the foresight or guidance to do. Here's the scenario:

Buying a house isn't that difficult, let's get that out of the way. Sure, there's a lot of paperwork you have to sign, and there is some work involved in finding a place to purchase, but we've bought 25 houses between the two of us in the past 8 years.

> *"The best way for a person to have happy thoughts is to count his blessings and not his cash."*
>
> ~Author Unknown

When you find the place you are interested in buying, it's best to go through a real estate agent to purchase the home (if you're new to the game). The realtor will help you schedule the inspection of the home, line up financing, and walk you through the process of closing on the property. You will most likely need someone to co-sign the loan unless you're making enough money to cover the mortgage on your own. (Keep in mind you'll be renting rooms to your buddies, so you may end up making positive rents on the property. The bank just wants to know that you can make the payment regardless of your dead-beat friends.) Having your parents co-sign the loan may give you a better interest rate in the long run. They've had longer to build up their credit history and got all the stupid mistakes behind them (hopefully).

The closing process can be somewhat stressful, oftentimes there are snags along the way because there are so many people involved in the transaction. Just be patient and know that things will work out as they should. Essentially during closing, you are signing documents agreeing to pay the mortgage on time, and authorizing a payoff from your lending company to the homeowners lending company. If the amount you are paying for the house is greater than what the homeowner owes on the place, he/she will get a check from the closing company for the "equity" in the home.

Now for the good part. Your "tenants" will pay you rent every month. In a perfect world, the total they pay is more than your monthly mortgage payment. In this case you have a positive cash flow on the property. You now own an asset. And just like the example from The Cashflow Quadrant, if your positive cash flow is enough to pay the monthly payment on a car, you are on your way to winning The Money Game!

Make Money While You Sleep

A good friend of ours owns a mini-storage company. Every month, regardless of his effort, he receives checks from the people that house their "treasures" in his little metal buildings. His plan from the beginning was to build these units, have them paid off in 15 years, and live off the income they'll generate for the rest of his life. At the current rental rates, if he never built another unit, he'd be able to live off of $9,000 a month in passive income.

Most Americans have heard from the time they were children, "Work hard, get a good job, buy a home and live the American dream." So people go to work every day trading hours for dollars. Do your 40 hours of chores a week and you'll get your corporate allowance. And people start figuring out what that corporate allowance will allow them to buy. Before they know it, they've become addicted to all the stuff they thought they needed (which is now housed in little metal buildings), and they have to continue getting their corporate allowance or they might lose their stuff.

"Create massive, passive, permanent streams of income."

~ Mark Victor Hansen

What we want you to understand is that you don't have to work hard all your life for money. At some point, we want your money to work harder than you do. Whether it's a mini-storage building, a rental property, stocks and bonds, or a row of gumball machines, figure out a way to put your money to work for you so that you make money while you sleep.

To illustrate how simple it can really be to make money while you sleep we purchased two gumball machines off of Ebay for $125 each. It cost $50 to get them shipped to our office. And we invested $50 in gumballs. Total investment: $350.

The machines were put in two different shopping malls just inside a popular t-shirt shop. Not expecting to make a fortune, we were shocked to find there was $90 between the two machines within the first month. Over the course of a year, the two machines made $1400 in profit. We ended up selling one on Craigslist for $375 and the other sits in our offices as a constant reminder to create passive income.

A new piece of technology like a cell phone might cost anywhere from $200-500. Doesn't it make more sense to invest that money in something that would pay for your cell phone over and over again every month?

What we want you to understand is it really is that easy. If you can get to the point where you make money while you sleep, you are on the path to winning The Money Game.

If you focus on buying stuff first, you'll never have assets. Focus instead on saving money to invest in assets. Eventually, your assets will buy you as much stuff as you could possibly want. And when you get all that stuff, we've got someone that can help you store it.

Key points:

- Assets put money in your pocket. Liabilities take money out.
- Invest in assets that pay you either now or in the future.
- Use your corporate allowance to buy assets not liabilities (i.e. "stuff").

Chapter Nine:

Monitor Your Progress

*"Budget:
a Mathematical
confirmation
of your suspicions."*

~ A.A. Latimer

There's a reality show on TV right now called "The Biggest Loser." The concept of the show involves teams of people who are trying to lose weight. Their combined loss at the end of the week determines who the winning team is and one of the "smallest" losers has to leave. What makes the show compelling for both the competitors and the people at home watching this, is the fact that they get to monitor their progress every single week. After being humiliated by trying to climb a staircase in a 74-floor building (a feat neither one of us could achieve), we then get to see that Freddy lost 3 pounds, Dave lost 4.5 pounds, Shirley lost 1 pound (she walked the steps), and DeeDee passed out on floor 15. As humans, we need to know the "score".

Think about if you went to a sporting event and there wasn't a scoreboard. It wouldn't be fun because you'd have no idea what the score was. Or what if the game was the fourth quarter and the scoreboard reflected the score back in the first quarter. It would be frustrating because you wouldn't have accurate numbers, and you wouldn't know if your team was winning or losing. When we are watching sporting events, we also want to know what the score is, or we always ask, "Who is winning?"

The point is we are infatuated with watching progress. Whether it's good progress or bad progress, we love to see it. So it is with your finances.

Take the example from Chapter 4 on Needs vs. Wants, the guy with $7,000 in credit card debt. His goal was to eliminate as much of his debt as possible right off the bat. By selling his CD and shoe collections he saw the balance decrease by

$3,800. His balance was then $3,200. He then got ambitious about paying off his credit card by the end of the year. By figuring out how much it would take each month to bring him to a zero balance, he plotted his plan of attack and took action. By consciously deciding that he had to make positive progress on his debt, he began focusing on how great it felt to get rid of the debt, instead of focusing on how great it felt to buy junk and store it in little metal buildings.

"I'd like to live as a poor man with lots of money."

~ Pablo Picasso

Spend More Time Reviewing Your Finances

Mark Victor Hansen and Robert Allen teamed up to write a book called The One-Minute Millionaire. It's a fantastic book written in two parts, so it's great for people who are more creative and want to read a story, and for people who are more analytical who just want the facts. One of the points they make in the book is that millionaires spend an extra few minutes on their finances every day. Some people say they don't have time to focus on their finances, but we're not talking about hours and hours of reconciling bank statements. It's an extra couple of minutes deciding whether or not you *really* need that pair of shoes you just picked up. It's an extra couple of minutes figuring out what you have left in your checkbook. If you really want to get serious about monitoring your progress, spend a few minutes a day on Quicken or some other financial software that helps you track your spending, saving, and investing. Just spend a little extra time every day and see the progress you're making.

In order to monitor your financial progress, obviously you need to have some defined money goals. For some, this may mean sticking within a budget and monitoring that closely. For others, it may mean determining by what day they want to have their debt paid. You may have a desired income goal for the month – or maybe you've been eyeing something in a store for some time and you're saving the money to pay cash for it. Whatever your money goals are, you must determine how long it will take you to reach those goals and strive every day/week/month to achieve them.

A fantastic savings site on the web is www.smartypig.com. Two entrepreneurs from Iowa figured out how to combine social media and banking and are making saving money cool again. The beauty of their site is you can specify what you're saving money for, and then send emails out to your friends and family letting them know what your goals are. Your network can actually contribute to your goals helping you reach them that much faster. Your grandparents won't believe their eyes! (But they WILL deposit money!)

Finally, make a commitment to yourself that you want to WIN The Money Game. Make a commitment to stick to your budget, to pay off your credit cards, to live within your means, and to pay cash for everything. If you need help staying accountable, ask a friend, family member, or co-worker to keep you on track. Sometimes it's nice to have someone checking in on your progress. If you should happen to falter or take a couple of steps back on your progress, re-commit to yourself that you WILL accomplish what you set out to do: WIN The Money Game!

Key points:

- If you don't know the score, how do you know if you're winning?
- Start monitoring your personal financial progress by tracking saving, spending, and investing.
- Commit yourself to winning The Money Game. Set goals immediately and start working to achieve them.

Chapter Ten:

Evaluate Yourself

"Do not value money
for any more
nor any less than
its worth; it is a good
servant but a
bad master."

~Alexandre Dumas fils,
Camille, 1852

One of the greatest things about this country is that we are all so different. Yet, isn't it interesting that we all begin to define success in the same way? Success is having it all: nice house, fancy cars, new clothes, dinners out, all the toys we won't ever play with. To us, it's completely obvious where we get these notions – it's all over television day and night.

The advertising geniuses in Chicago and New York have figured Americans out. They come up with tag lines like, "There are some things money can't buy, for everything else there's....." (Fill in the next word). SEE?! Whether you believe that statement or not, subconsciously, your mind says, "it's okay if you don't have money for that – there are some things money can't buy, but for ***everything*** else, put it on your MasterCard."

Every day you see thousands of marketing messages telling you what success is. Think about the vision of success you see on MTV's show Cribs. Multiple expensive cars, mansions, all the bling you can imagine – what they don't tell you is half of these rappers live paycheck to paycheck. Show me 20 rappers with recording contracts and I'll show you 10 who have a negative net-worth. They OWE more than they OWN!

The point is don't rely on someone else's version of success when defining your own. Especially financial success! Don't get us wrong, we work hard daily to improve our lifestyle (and we must admit life is pretty good right now). We have a lot of "stuff" that others want but we have all those things because we can pay for them, and we NEVER sacrifice our financial success to get them. It's absolutely essential to evaluate yourself about what's important to you financially. By taking the time to determine what you truly want in life, and what your beliefs are about money, only then will you be prepared to make some of the difficult (and not-so-difficult) choices about how to live your life.

You've heard the saying "Keeping up with the Joneses?" This concept is what causes people to put all their *wants* in their *need* category. People see their neighbors driving a new Lexus and think, "if HE can afford a Lexus, WE should be driving one." It's a race to prove who has the newest, best, fastest, or most expensive toys. The problem with this is it's a loser's race if you aren't evaluating yourself along the way. Too many people decide to "keep up with the Joneses" and stretch themselves to the point that now they're putting groceries and gas on their credit cards because they are out of money at the end of every month.

"Car sickness is the feeling you get when the monthly payment is due."

~ Author Unknown

In Texas they have a saying for people who appear to have it all but in reality have nothing: Big Hat, No Cattle. In the past, ranchers who had a large piece of property and lots of cattle wore bigger hats than everyone else. In fact, the size of your hat determined how successful you really were. Overtime, the "look" of being successful (big hats) started getting popular, but ranchers didn't have the land or cattle to back it up. So the next time you see someone in their teens or early 20's driving a flashy car, think to yourself: Big Hat, No Cattle!

Now, we don't want you to think less of a young person driving a fancy car – maybe their parents bought it for them or they may have scrimped and saved in high school to pay for that car. If that's the case, great for them! What we want you to understand is as you look around and see what other people have, you must keep in mind that, especially in college, your friends are as broke as you. It shouldn't be about showing off a $70 pair of jeans you bought at Abercrombie, it should be about showing off a $2 pair of jeans you bought at Goodwill that look just as good. Yeah, your friends may call you cheap, but the $68 dollars you saved could be the start of a gigantic investment portfolio. It could be the beginning of a real estate empire. At the very least, it's $68 you have and they don't. And let's face it, you've both got denim covering your ass-ets.

One of the things you should be crystal clear about is what you want to accomplish financially in your life. Right now, it may not seem like you have a great deal to invest or save. If that's the case, we challenge you to find $20 a month that you can put in your "go to hell" fund. Maybe your goals include being able to afford a car when you graduate. Do you want to get into real estate? If so, start saving now, and learn what you'll need to do to succeed in that business.

You also need to be crystal clear about your beliefs around money. Here are some of ours:

Life will pay any price you ask of it. Some people just don't ask for enough.

Living on credit cards is a sure-fire way to LOSE The Money Game.

Cash is king - don't buy anything but houses or cars that you can't pay cash for.

A little every month will grow to a lot over time.

We must understand how interest works both for us and against us.

Delayed gratification is the best investment you'll ever make.

We will never sacrifice our needs for our wants.

Key points:

- You must identify what your version of financial success is.
- Keeping up with the Joneses is a sure-fire way to lose TMG.
- Be crystal clear of your beliefs around money.

Chapter Eleven:

Putting It All Together

"A nickel ain't worth a dime anymore."

~Yogi Berra

As you have read this book, we have taken you through the rules to Winning The Money Game. Now, as you finish this book, we are going to end it exactly how we started by challenging you to put these rules into action. Build the right habits and more importantly, break the wrong ones.

Remember, it's not always the popular choices you need to make in order to win TMG. And while society sometimes looks down on people who don't have the finer things, a lot of people with the finer things in life are struggling just to pay the bills. Meanwhile, others who don't "look" successful according to society are doing what it takes to win the game.

We have talked about:

Making Saving and Investing Money
Ongoing Savings
Needs vs. Wants
Essential Money Skills
Your Money Choices and Their Consequences
Grow with Your Money
Assets vs. Liabilities
Monitor Your Progress
Evaluate Yourself

We wish you the best of luck as you begin the path to winning The Money Game. It's said that money doesn't buy you happiness, and we can attest that being broke won't either. Winning the money game is a lot better than losing it!

Have fun and enjoy life to the fullest, but don't sacrifice your financial life to do it. Create assets, and then use your money to buy everything you want. We encourage you to continue to look in the mirror from time to time and be honest with yourself. Ask the question: Am I doing what it takes to win The Money Game? If you are, give yourself a pat on the back. If you're not, kick yourself in the backside and change your ways!

Use this book as a reference and a frequent check up on your situation. Good luck and remember, life is better when you are winning The Money Game.

About The Authors

Adam Carroll

Adam Carroll's entrepreneurial spirit came shining through at the age of 7 when he decided to start a business selling cakes door-to-door. Though the business was very short-lived, in a week's time, Adam managed to sell two cakes and make a profit of $17. He was hooked. While in college, Adam and his cousin founded ACB Enterprises, a vending company whose featured products were the Hollywood Pop popcorn machines new to the Midwest. The business helped fund some of his college adventures and gave him a business education no formal curriculum could provide. After college, Adam followed his true passion of public speaking and delivered a motivational message to tens of thousands of high school and college students nationwide. It was during this time that Adam and Chad created the concept of a financial literacy presentation that not only educated, but entertained and energized students to take a positive step with their financial lives.

While coaching small business owners through the E-Myth Mastery Program, Adam was offered a job as Vice President of Sales and Marketing for a small consulting company in central Texas. His experience with business owners led Adam to formally partner with Chad and "The Money Game" was created. The company that delivers the message is now known as National Financial Educators. Adam's passion is helping people live the life they were destined to live by taking control of their finances once and for all.

In 2007, Adam witnessed what was happening in the mortgage industry and decided to create the first socially-responsible mortgage company in the Midwest. Four Legacies Mortgage is his education-based mortgage company that focuses on helping people take control of their finances by paying off debt, reducing expenses, and optimizing the use of their largest asset, their home. The Four Legacies in order are: Financial Freedom, Time Freedom, Relationship Freedom, and Service Freedom. >>

About The Authors

Adam has delivered The Money Game to over 150,000 college students from one coast to another and everywhere in between. The most gratifying part of the program is the feedback from students (sometimes a year or two later) who say it literally changed the way they looked at their finances.

Adam's true purpose is to help others create the lives they've always desired, but were never able to afford.

About The Authors

Chad Carden

Chad Carden was born into the speaking world, his father a well-known speaker and trainer. Having grown up around some of the greats in the industry, at a very young age Chad made a decision that this is what he wanted to do most in life. When Chad graduated college he was in the same position that faces 90% of college graduates – in debt, making very little money and not a clue how to improve his situation. Chad learned quickly with the help of 2 very influential mentors, and achieved success delivering sales training to Fortune 100 companies. Through focus and discipline, Chad paid off his debts and began growing his net worth. He now lives debt free, and enjoys the opportunity to teach people not to make the same mistakes he did. At a very young age Chad has had the opportunity to speak to over 100,000 people >>

and consult with companies such as Morgan Stanley, UBS, Enterprise Rent-A-Car, Farmers Insurance, Merrill Lynch, and many others.

Chad wants to send the message to young adults to enjoy life to the fullest and at the same time make sure you are setting yourself up for success in all areas of your life. Chad has a unique and entertaining presentation style and an ability to relate to any audience. He is a student of people and strives to learn something new every day. Chad is truly living a dream doing what he loves, changing people's lives, having fun, learning and teaching!

About National Financial Educators

National Financial Educators was founded to educate young people in high school and college on issues of making, saving and spending money. Their mission is to educate, entertain, and inspire young people to make better choices financially, by providing students the information they need in a format they accept. They believe money should not be a taboo subject and approach the topic with honesty, sincerity, and with a healthy dose of humor. NFE has a mission and that is to change the fate of the nation's young people by giving them the knowledge they need to make sound decisions when handling money. From controlling overspending to understanding needs and wants, their goal is to create a more financially solid future for America.

Everyone that speaks for NFE has a passion for this topic and are doing what it takes to win their own personal money game. They currently have 10 speakers across the country either living debt free or on their way to living debt free, by applying the very same rules taught in the programs listed below. NFE has spoken to students at over 500 schools and has profoundly changed to way students look at money. They continue to bring the message of financial literacy to schools across the country and are growing everyday. NFE wants to make sure that every student possible hears this message. The following pages outline the programs offered.

"The Money Game"

"The Money Game – If You Want to Win, You Better Know the Rules" is a 60-minute presentation developed by National Financial Educators. The program is geared to help educate students on financial issues like the perils of credit card debt, spending less than you earn, automatic investing, and protecting your credit, to name a few.

Through real-life stories and examples, The Money Game will impact students in ways no college or high school class could! Both educational and entertaining, students will be involved on-stage and in the audience to gain maximum impact of the message.

The handouts students will receive are part of a blended learning concept. By actively listening, filling out the workbooks, and participating in exercises, no matter what the student's learning style, they have got it covered. "The Money Game" is not just educational and motivational; it's just plain fun!

Students will also have the option of signing up for a free monthly newsletter that provides continuous financial support and information. The newsletter covers topics like finding scholarships, minimizing credit card debt and building assets.

Here is "The Money Game" broken down:

- Making and Saving Money
- Ongoing Saving and Investing Money
- Needs Vs Wants
- Essential Money Skills
- Your Money Choices and Their Consequences

"Financial Freedom Weekend"

NFE is also expanding the way they reach students by holding in-depth money retreats across the country. In these retreats you will get:

An in-depth look at your own situation
How to change your spending habits
A breakdown on different investments
What investments are right for you

AND LOTS MORE!!

The Financial Freedom Weekends are held in different locations and are usually in a two day format. Students have to opportunity to take an in-depth look at their own situation, as well as get a look at true life examples of people who have turned their situations around. When students leave the Financial Freedom Weekend they will have all the tools they need to build a life full of financial success. These retreats will help truly change the way people look at money.

Corporate Programs

What would it be like if every employee in your company were financially literate? Studies report that as much as 65% of an employee's workday is consumed by money worries. What if you could recoup even 25% of the time spent worrying about money? More and more companies across the country are beginning to understand that financially stable employees means less turnover, higher productivity, and more profit.

While every corporate situation is unique, we'll customize the content of the program to adequately cover your company's employee concerns. It's said that your employees are the only appreciating asset your company has – shouldn't you invest in them too?

About National Financial Educators

For more information on any of these programs, please contact NFE!

National Financial Educators
1031 Office Park Road, Suite 1
West Des Moines, IA 50265
(515) 223-2343
www.nationalfinancialeducators.com

Other Topics

The founders of National Financial Educators and authors of "Winning The Money Game", Adam Carroll and Chad Carden, also speak on other topics to help people really see their full potential in all areas of life.

For more information about any of these topics please contact NFE at the information below:

Financial Topics

The Money Game — Helping students set themselves up for success, not failure, when it comes to their personal finances.

The Way Of The Entrepreneur — Running a successful business from A to Z

Leadership Topics

Who's Working Harder, You or Your Business? — What 5 things are keeping your business from really thriving

Leadership Training — Grow your people & grow your business, the six C's of Leadership

Team Building — The importance of an effective team within your organization

Other Topics

Conflict Resolution — The importance of dealing with conflicts effectively

Motivating Yourself and Others — It is one of the most important aspects of your job

Dealing with Negative People — They are out there, so how to effectively deal with them

Networking P.O.W.E.R. — Your dream job and greatest aspirations may be closer than you think.

Professional/Personal Development Topics:

Vision to Reality- Make your vision a reality by focusing on the prize

*Using P.E.P.P to Keep Life in Order-*A real look at how to deal with life situations both personally and professionally.

Sales Training- How to make the sale using the consultative approach

Stress Management- Controlling Stress and Worry

Giving an Effective Presentation- Whether it is a five minute talk or an eight hour program: The Fundamentals

Other Topics

Self-Confidence- Believing in you is the key

Communication Skills- Communication is a two way street

Attitude- You choose your attitude everyday, and that is vital to your way of life

Enthusiasm- One major key to success

Adjusting to Change- Adapting to change is one major key to survival

Time Management- If you don't control time, time will control you

Comfort Zones- Creating the ability to expand your comfort zones for positive movement

National Financial Educators
1031 Office Park Road, Suite 1
West Des Moines, IA 50265
(515) 223-2343
www.nationalfinancialeducators.com